BEIJING
AND
XI'AN

CHINA'S GREAT CAPITALS

HUGH LAUTER LEVIN ASSOCIATES, INC.

Beijing and Xi'an

© 2000 Hugh Lauter Levin Associates, Inc.

Written and Coordinated by: Charles Schoenfeld
Photo Research & Factual Editing: the staff of China Pictorial
Factual Editing: China Travel & Tourism Press
Executive Factual Editor: Gong Weijian, CTTP
Copyediting: Ou Xiaomei and Amy Zindell

Design: Dana Levy, Perpetua Press, Los Angeles

ISBN: 0-88363-159-8

Printed in Hong Kong
Published and distributed in China by China Travel and Tourism Press

http://www.HLLA.com

Contents

Beijing

The Great Wall at the Gold Mountain	8
Peking Man	11
A Watchtower in the Forbidden City	12
Tiananmen Gate	12
The Forbidden City	19
A Gilded Bronze Lion in front of Qianqing Gate	20
The Imperial Garden	23
Phoenix Coronet of an Empress	24
Imperial Throne in the Hall of Supreme Harmony	27
The Summer Palace	28
The Long Corridor	31
Taihe Gate	32
Suzhou Street	37
The Marble Boat	38
The Temple of Heaven	41
Caisson Ceiling of the Imperial Vault of Heaven	42
Beihai Park	45
Ming Tombs	46
Eastern Qing Tombs	49
The Hall of Prayer for Good Harvests	50
Xinhuamen, Front Gate of Zhongnanhai	55
Ten Ferries	56
Tanzhe Temple	59
Ancient Observatory	60
Ruins of Yuanmingyuan	63
Traditional Housing	64
China Central Television Tower	67
Jingxinzhai (Tranquil Heart Study)	68
Grand View Garden	73
Beijing Roast Duck	74
Beijing West Railway Station	77

Xi'an

Mount Huashan	80
The Ruins of Banpo Village	83
Terra-Cotta Warriors	84
The Mausoleum of Emperor Qin Shihuang	87
Terra-Cotta Archer in Qin Shihuang's Mausoleum	88
Bronze Chariot from Qin Shihuang's Mausoleum	91
Maoling Mausoleum	92
Qianling Tomb	95
Maiji Grottoes	96
City Wall	96
Huaqing Hot Springs	103
Ladies-in-Waiting Mural, Tomb of Princess Yongtai	104
Honor Guard Mural, Tomb of Crown Prince Yide	107
Han Dynasty Bronze Horse	108
Tomb of the Yellow Emperor	111
The Great Mosque	112
Famen Temple Pagoda	115
Water and Land Nunnery	116
Temple of Flourishing Buddhism	120
Lesser Wild Goose Pagoda	121
The Bell Tower	123
Forest of Steles	124

BEIJING

The Great Wall at the Gold Mountain

WHEN THE SPACE SHUTTLE APOLLO 11 made the first manned lunar landing, it was reported that the Great Wall of China was the only man-made structure easily visible from space with the naked eye.

Listed among the Seven Wonders of the Ancient World, the Great Wall stretches over 4,000 miles, rising and falling with the undulating terrain, traversing mountain ridges, vast deserts, and grasslands. If the earth, stones, and bricks making up the wall were used to construct a smaller wall, only five meters high and one meter thick, that wall could circle the globe at the equator.

When China was made up of small, independent kingdoms, during the period from 770 to 221 B.C., the rulers of those kingdoms built walls to defend their own lands from nomadic tribes outside their borders, as well as from one another. Then, in 221 B.C., when Qin Shi Huang, the founding emperor of the Qin Dynasty, unified China under his own rule, he conscripted men above the age of fifteen to join these separate walls into a single, longer structure. Legend tells many tales of the anguish suffered by the families of these conscripted workers. Later dynasties—most notably the Han (206 B.C.–A.D. 220) and the Ming (A.D. 1368-1644)—extended the wall and added battlements, guard towers, and sentry posts.

Several sections of the Great Wall, particularly those built under the Ming Dynasty, still stand intact in the outskirts of Beijing, testifying to the high quality of construction during that period. The sections of the wall at Jinshanling, Badaling, Mutianyu, and Simatai are some of the best-known, and most attractive to tourists. The Jinshanling section of the wall, built along the ridge of a mountain to give Chinese soldiers the advantage of high terrain when resisting invading armies, is capped with towers in different styles—sixty-seven can be found within a 10-kilometer stretch. The most impressive of these is the Storehouse Tower, which was used as a garrison headquarters and is protected by special defensive barriers and an extra wall 60 meters downhill. The grandiose Badaling section of the wall is 8.5 meters high, and rests on a foundation of granite blocks weighing 1,000 kilograms each. Ten people can walk shoulder-to-shoulder across the pathway on top. The section near Gubeikou, north of Beijing, is sometimes thought to be the most scenically impressive part of the entire wall.

Peking Man

ZHOUKOUDIAN VILLAGE is located in the suburbs of Beijing, about 48 kilometers southwest of the city. The area is famous for the excavation site in the nearby limestone hills and caves, where archaeologists uncovered the largest collection of *Homo erectus* fossils ever found at any single location, and named their discovery Peking Man. Altogether, some fourteen partial crania, eleven mandibles, 147 teeth, and numerous limbs and stone tools were catalogued between the years of 1929 and 1937. These are believed to be the remnants of at least forty individuals.

Homo erectus was an ancestor of modern man, who lived between 1.8 million and 200,000 years ago. His skull, with its large molars and heavy brow, was similar to that of his predecessor, *Homo habilis*. However, evidence indicates that his tools were more sophisticated than those of *habilis*, and that he was able to control fire. The cave at Zhoukoudian, in fact, with its charred animal bones and a firepit with ash as deep as seven feet, represents the world's earliest incidence of the controlled use of fire. A bone needle, shells, and stone beads at the site suggest also that Peking Man made clothing from animal skins. The knowledge that Peking Man developed a rudimentary civilization, made clothing, controlled fire, hunted large animals, and cooked his food provides valuable insight into the life of a human ancestor.

Peking Man, who inhabited the caves at Zhoukoudian intermittently from 460,000 to 230,000 years ago, also represents an important rung of the evolutionary ladder. The shape of Peking Man's skull is an intermediate step between neanderthal and modern man, a link previously missing. Indeed, some researchers have tried to claim that *Homo erectus Pekinensis* was not a human ancestor at all, but merely a monkey—a claim rendered instantly ridiculous by placing the skull next to that of an actual monkey.

The Peking Man skull pictured here—which is actually a female skull, despite the name—is not one of the original discoveries. Those fossils were lost at sea in 1941, while being transported for safekeeping to the American Museum of Natural History in anticipation of Japanese aggression. Fortunately, the German anatomist Franz Weidenreich had already made exacting casts of the fossils, and extensive illustrated documentation. Weidenreich's casts are now in use in scientific institutions around the world.

A Watchtower over the Forbidden City (Opposite)

THE FORBIDDEN CITY IN BEIJING, where the twenty-four emperors of the Ming and Qing dynasties lived, held court, and ruled the country, is impressively defended—surrounded by a perimeter wall thirty-three feet high and three kilometers in length, and encircled by a moat fifty-two meters wide and 3,800 meters long, named Outer Golden Water River. There is also an inner moat, named, appropriately enough, Inner Golden Water River, which winds around through the inside of the Forbidden City. With a watchtower such as the one pictured here crowning each of the four corners of the palace enclosure, the palace looks like a carefully defended castle.

The tranquil surface of the moat reflects the silhouette of the watchtower, which reminds the viewer that even when Chinese architects built a structure for defense, they never neglected considerations of beauty. Each of the four towers is unique in design, but each was built with nine beams and eighteen pillars and topped with six hipped and gabled roofs. The three-tiered eaves sloping into twenty-eight upturning curves, along with ten gables and seventy-two roof ridges, make the towers as graceful as they are functional.

According to legend, the artisans responsible for building the towers spent days and nights in anguish, unable to come up with a suitable design. Then the long-deceased master carpenter Lu Ban of the Spring and Autumn period (770–476 B.C.) returned to the world, and walked past the construction site carrying a grasshopper cage in his hand. Given this inspiration, the designers finally were able to design and build the four towers to the requisite standard of elegance.

Tiananmen Gate (Overleaf)

TIANANMEN SQUARE IS THE LARGEST public square in the world, and can hold as many as one million people. Traditional town planning in China did not allow for places where the masses could gather, so the square is a relatively recent addition to Beijing's landscape. It was created when imperial offices along the royal path between the Forbidden City and the Temple of Heaven were demolished.

In the center of the square is the Monument to the People's Heroes. To the west is the Great Hall of the People, and to the east are the Museum of Chinese History and the Museum of the Chinese Revolution. At the southern end of the square is the Memorial Hall of Chairman Mao Zedong. And to the north is the oldest structure on the square—Tiananmen Gate, the front entrance to the Imperial Palace, known to Westerners as the Forbidden City.

Tiananmen Gate (The Gate of Heavenly Peace) was constructed in 1417, during the reign of the Ming emperor Yongle. It stands 33.7 meters high, and covers an area of over 20,000 square meters. There are five passageways through the gate. In ancient times, the central passageway was reserved for the Emperor.

Two pairs of *huabiao*—ornamental pillars of marble—stand near the gate, one in front and one behind. Atop each pillar sits an animal known as a *kong*, expert at keeping watch. The southern pair face away from the Forbidden City, and are known as *wangjungui,* meaning "watching for the Emperor's return." The northern pair face toward the palace, and are called *wangjunchu,* or "watching the Emperor's progress."

Today, Tiananmen Gate is an important icon in China; its image appears on banknotes, policemen's caps, and many state documents. In October of 1949, Mao Zedong proclaimed the founding of the People's Republic from the same tower that Ming and Qing emperors used when issuing edicts. Mao's portrait still hangs over the central passageway, and the entrance is flanked by two slogans: "Long Live the People's Republic of China," and "Long Live the Great Union between the Peoples of the World."

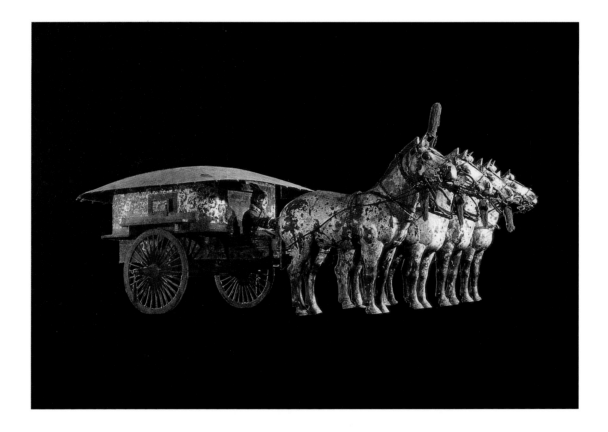

Bronze Chariot from Qin Shi Huang's Mausoleum

Xi'an

THE BRONZE CHARIOTS unearthed alongside the terra-cotta army at the mausoleum of Qin Shi Huang are so impressive that when Queen Elizabeth II of England visited Xi'an in 1987, the Chinese presented her with an exact duplicate of one chariot as a gift.

The discovery of the bronze chariots began in 1978, when archaeologists found a gold ornament roughly the size of a golf ball. By December of 1980, the two chariots had been entirely excavated. The pit that held them was seven meters long, 2.3 meters wide, 7.5 meters deep, and enclosed on all six sides by planks of wood, so that it resembled a giant coffin. The chariots were positioned one behind the other, facing west. Today, the chariots are on display toward the left side of the hangar that protects the terra-cotta warriors. Photos of the chariots' excavation adorn the walls of the exhibition chamber.

Each chariot is drawn by four horses, and includes a driver, also cast in bronze. The chariots demonstrate the skill of Qin metalworkers. Most fittings are of solid bronze, and the harness and reins are inlaid with gold and silver. Each chariot has a bronze canopy, cast very thin but remarkably smooth and even. The drivers are rendered in fine detail, their hair filed to represent individual strands, their postures and the lines of their clothing tele-graphing their next movements. The horses, too, with their bulging muscles, flared nostrils, and cocked ears, seem ready to leap into action.

The first carriage is 2.25 meters long including the horses, and is believed to be half the size of its real-life counterpart. The canopy suggests that this chariot was designed as a pleasure conveyance; a military chariot would have had no canopy, as such an accessory would only have limited the soldiers' mobility.

The second carriage, pictured here, was called an *anche,* or safe chariot. Such carriages had been used by kings, dukes, and other nobles since the Zhou Dynasty. Its roof is lower than that of the first chariot, and extends forward over the driver to provide shade. The occupant could only see out through rhomboidal lattice windows, and could hardly be seen at all from the outside. Silk fragments found inside the chariot attest to its luxury.

These bronze chariots are a reminder that the Qin people had always been fond of horses, and known for their skill as drivers, since before the founding of the Qin Dynasty. In the past, the Qin people had driven carriages for the nobles of other dynasties, and in the State of Qin, they would compose songs praising their favorite horses and carriages.

Maoling Mausoleum

Xi'an

L OCATED ABOUT FORTY-FIVE KILOMETERS west of Xi'an, Maoling Mausoleum is a huge green mound nestled dramatically among the hills of Shaanxi Province. It is the largest of the more than twenty Han Dynasty tombs in the region, and took more than fifty years to build. Remarkably, the entire construction took place during the reign of its eventual occupant, Emperor Wudi (140–87 B.C.), whose fifty-four-year stint on the throne was the longest of any emperor in Chinese history.

Maoling Mausoleum is notable among the imperial tombs of China not only for its architectural splendor and its precious collection of cultural relics, but also because it houses the remains of an emperor who left behind a legacy every bit as grand as his tomb. The sixth emperor of the Han Dynasty (206 B.C.–A.D. 220), Emperor Wudi, born Liu Che, was made crown prince at the age of seven, and ascended the throne at the age of sixteen. He and the first Qin emperor are usually cited as the two most responsible for the consolidation of centralized political power in ancient China.

It was Qin Shi Huang who unified the individual states of the Warring States Period, but Emperor Wudi later deprived the several hundred princes and other nobles who still held local power of their noble titles. He also reserved the right to mint coins for the central government alone, and established a property tax on businessmen and industrialists. He established an Imperial College to train government officials, and, to unify the Chinese way of thinking, he decreed that Confucianism should be the only accepted philosophy in China. He died at the age of seventy-one, leaving behind a stronger nation.

Emperor Wudi's mausoleum is a trapezoidal structure over 46 meters high and 240 meters long. There are vestiges of a surrounding wall some 400 meters long and nearly 6 meters thick, including watchtowers in the east, west, and north. The grounds are covered in flowers, and decorated with a large fountain. The many relics found in the tomb include a full jade burial suit, which was believed to preserve the body from decay.

The mausoleum grounds include twelve smaller tombs belonging to favored court officials and concubines. This photo shows the tomb of the general Huo Qubing (140–117 B.C.), a brilliant strategist and brave warrior who conducted multiple campaigns against the northern (Hun) tribes. Huo Qubing died at the age of twenty-four, and his tomb—which features ceramic figurines, giant stone statues, eave tiles and other relics, is considered one of the more splendid satellite tombs at Maoling.

Qianling Tomb

Xi'an

THE TOMBS OF THE TANG Dynasty (A.D. 618–907) are located in Shaanxi Province, just six kilometers north of Qianxian County, and eighty kilometers northwest of modern Xi'an. Of all the Tang tombs, the largest and most splendid is Qianling Mausoleum, the resting place of Emperor Gaozong (628–683) and his wife, Empress Wu Zetian (624–705). Wu Zetian is one of the three women rulers in Chinese history, and the only one to hold the title of Emperor, which she took over upon the death of her husband.

The twenty-three-year period of construction required to complete Qianling began in 684. The tomb's main buildings are situated on the slope of Liangshan Hill's northern peak, the tallest of Liangshan's three peaks. The eastern and western peaks stand nearby, attractively framing the central peak. The mausoleum grounds were originally enclosed by an inner and an outer protective wall, but the outer wall collapsed long ago. The inner wall, with a circumference of forty kilometers, surrounds a total area of about 240 hectares, and includes four gates: the Blue Dragon Gate in the east, the White Tiger Gate in the west, the Tortoise Gate in the north, and the Phoenix Gate in the south. Qianling also includes seventeen satellite tombs of Tang princes and ministers.

The *shendao* (divine path) leading through the grounds of Qianling passes some interesting sights. The road itself is lined with stone sculptures of winged horses, ostriches, ordinary horses, and human figures, arranged in pairs. Qianling served as a model for the type and arrangement of sculptures placed at the tombs of later emperors.

There are two stone tablets near the southern gate, each 6.3 meters high. The one on the western side of the gate is a monument to Emperor Gaozong, with eight thousand words of praise written by Empress Wu Zetian. The tablet is divided into seven segments, representing the seven Elements: Earth, Fire, Water, Wood, Metal, the Sun, and the Moon. The eastern tablet is the famous Wordless Stele, erected by Wu Zetian in her own memory. The only one of its kind, the Wordless Stele is a testament to the empress's legendary arrogance—it signifies that her greatness could not be expressed in words.

Not far from these tablets is the field of stone statues of foreign envoys and minority chieftains who attended Emperor Gaozong's funeral. There were originally sixty-one of these statues; one has disappeared, and all but two of the remaining sixty have been beheaded by political vandals.

Maiji Grottoes (Opposite)

Gansu Province, near Xi'an

SOME OF THE FINEST EXAMPLES of ancient art in China take the form of statuary grottoes and caves, hewn into the faces of cliffs and mountains. These sites, which typically contain vast painted murals, stone and clay statues, and decorative paving tiles and pillars, can vary greatly in size–ranging from thirty centimeters to more than thirty meters in height. The murals and sculptures are usually representations of Buddha or depictions of stories from Buddhist history.

The Maiji Grottoes are located in southwest Gansu Province, thirty kilometers southeast of Tianshui County and 350 kilometers southeast of Gansu's capital city, Lanzhou. The grottoes are close-knit layers of caves, hewn into the relatively soft stone of Maiji (Wheat Stack) Mountain, whose name derives from its shape, said to resemble a stack of wheat.

Work on the grottoes began in the late West Jin Dynasty, and continued over a span of many centuries, from the Northern Wei through the Qing dynasties. Today, there are more than 190 caves and grottoes carved into the mountain. These contain some 7,000 statues made of stone and clay, and more than 1,300 square meters (14,000 square feet) of mural paintings. While the statues are predominantly Buddhist in theme, the murals provide interesting depictions of ancient architecture and ritual in China.

One of the most striking and uncommon properties of the Maiji Mountain Grottoes is their daunting height and location. Many are situated on prohibitively sheer crags and cliff faces, frequently as high as thirty meters off the ground, and some as much as eighty meters high. The grottoes are linked by paths made of wooden planks, and part of the excitement of seeing the grottoes comes in travelling along these paths.

City Wall (Overleaf)

Xi'an

LONG BEFORE ZHU YUANZHANG had founded the Ming Dynasty, a wise hermit named Zhu Sheng advised him to "build high walls, store abundant provisions, and take your time in proclaiming yourself emperor." Zhu Yuanzhang followed this advice, and when he had finally unified the country, he ordered many cities to build protective walls. Of all the ancient city walls in China, Xi'an's is the largest and best preserved.

Xi'an's city wall had existed since the Yuan Dynasty. The original wall was made of earth, rammed layer upon layer. When Xi'an once again became an important political and commercial center during the Ming Dynasty, the emperors had the wall rebuilt. Its surface was fortified with gray bricks, and it was built up to be 12 to 15 meters high, and 12 to 14 meters wide across the top.

The wall was designed to be defensible. There are 5,984 crenellations along its length, with arrow holes directly beneath. Spaced every 120 meters along the wall are ninety-eight ramparts, their tops level with the height of the wall, each with a sentry building on top. There are also watchtowers at each of the wall's four corners. The ramparts on top of the corner watchtowers are larger than those along the body of the wall, due to the strategic importance of the corners. Along the inside of the outer walls are parapets, to prevent soldiers from falling off the top.

The north, south, east, and west gates each have three towers: one for raising and lowering a drawbridge, one for soldiers with bows and arrows, and an inner tower through which one entered the city. Today, a circular park has been built between the wall and the moat. Its trees and flowers add to the beauty of Xi'an.

Temple of Flourishing Buddhism

Xi'an

X UANZANG, BORN CHEN HUI, was a famous Buddhist monk who lived in China in the seventh century, during the Tang Dynasty. Secure in his devotion to the Buddhist faith from an early age, he became a monk at the age of thirteen. When he was twenty-eight years old, he left China on a pilgrimage to India, determined to bring back Buddhist scriptures from their land of origin. His journey is the basis for a folk tale called *The Journey to the West*, which is well-known even today. The story has been performed as an opera, written in the form of children's books, and produced as a feature-length cartoon.

Upon his return to China's capital city of Chang'an many years later, at the age of forty-four, Xuanzang set about translating from Sanskrit into Chinese the Buddhist scriptures that he had collected in India. The Greater Wild Goose Pagoda, in the Temple of Mercy and Benevolence, was built as his place of study, and a repository for his manuscripts. He translated some 1,335 volumes of scriptures, wrote an important book called *Records of Travel in the Western Region,* and is credited with the creation of the Faxiang sect of Buddhism. During his lifetime, he was honored within the Buddhist faith as a Master of Sanzang.

Xuanzang died in A.D. 664, at the age of sixty-five. He was buried on the Bailu Plain, east of Xi'an. Xingjiaosi, the Temple of Flourishing Buddhism, was built to house his ashes and *sarira,* or skeletal remains. Construction of the temple was completed in 669, five years after his death, and his remains were moved there.

The temple is situated on the side of a hill near the Fan River, overlooking a village and the wide Shaoling Plain. At the center of the temple is a large square pagoda, beneath which lie Xuanzang's remains. Two smaller stupas to either side of the main one mark the resting places of his two most favored disciples. In a pavilion beside these stupas is the original stone figurine of Xuanzang carrying his traveling pack on his back, looking cheerful. This sculpture is often copied, and is perhaps the best-known image of Xuanzang. Over the entrance to the temple are the two Chinese characters meaning "Flourishing Buddhism," in the calligraphy of a Tang emperor.

Lesser Wild Goose Pagoda

Xi'an

XUANZANG WAS A renowned Buddhist monk from China who spent eighteen years in the mid-seventh century on a pilgrimage to India studying Buddhism. When he returned from India in the year 652, the emperor sent a large delegation to welcome his party, and the entire city of Xi'an celebrated his return. Since Xuanzang had brought manuscripts of Buddhist scriptures home with him, to translate them into Chinese, Emperor Gaozong of the Tang Dynasty (618–907) ordered the construction of the Greater Wild Goose (Dayan) Pagoda within the Temple of Mercy and Benevolence (Da Ci'en) to house these manuscripts. The construction of the pagoda was a political move meant to entice Xuanzang into becoming the head of the temple.

The Lesser Wild Goose Pagoda is a part of Jianfu Temple, to the south of West Friendship Road in Xi'an. It was built in 707, the third year of the reign of Emperor Zhongzong of the Tang Dynasty. Like the Greater Wild Goose Pagoda, its layers of bricks have no mortar or cement between them. It is only fifty meters high, compared to the sixty-four meters of the Greater Wild Goose Pagoda, but has fifteen stories–eight more than its taller counterpart.

The huge bell in the pagoda's tower–4.5 meters high and weighing ten tons–is known as the Magic Bell. An old legend has it that if one wrote a note on a piece of yellow paper, addressed to loved ones living far away, the chiming of the bell would pass the message along to them. The bell is inscribed with wishes such as: "Long live the Emperor," and "May Buddhist principles prevail."

In 1487, a massive earthquake opened a one-foot crack in the pagoda from top to bottom. Then, in 1521, a second quake actually *closed* that crack. The people referred to the incident as the Magic Healing of the pagoda. This "magical" event was due to the hemispherical shape of the pagoda's foundation–a brilliant piece of workmanship on the part of the ancient craftsmen who built it.

The Bell Tower

FOR CENTURIES, ever since the Ming Dynasty (1368–1644), bell towers and drum towers have appeared prominently in many cities throughout China.

The tolling of the great bells and the beating of the drums kept time for the city each day, and could also be used to sound alarms. The bell in the Bell Tower announced the time every morning, and the drum in the Drum Tower gave the time every evening; therefore, they were known as the "morning bell" and the "dusk drum." Eventually, the practice of using the drum in the evening was discontinued, and the drum was reserved solely for warning the people of emergencies in time of war.

Though many Chinese cities have bell towers, nowhere is such a structure as spectacular, or as significant a symbol of the town, as in Xi'an. Xi'an's bell tower is taller than any other in the country, and was built earlier. The Bell Tower was first erected in 1384, in the Yingxiang Temple, which was then located at the city's geographic center. By 1582, the city had expanded, and so the tower was moved to its current location at the city's new center, where the North, South, East, and West streets meet. It has been repaired three times since 1949, to keep it in perfect condition. The Drum Tower is located a short distance to the northwest of the Bell Tower.

The building is 36 meters tall, made of bricks and wood. Although its interior is only two stories high, there are three stories of eaves on the exterior. The eaves are supported by brackets mounted on the tops of columns and crossbeams–a unique Chinese architectural style known as *dougong*. The tower sits on a square-shaped base of blue bricks, 8.6 meters high and 35.5 meters across.

Legend tells that after an enormous dragon caused a series of devastating earthquakes in the plains of Shaanxi Province, the governor of Xi'an ordered the construction of a giant chain to imprison the dragon beneath the city. He then had the Bell Tower constructed to weigh down the dragon and prevent its escape. Though metaphorical, the legend may have some basis in fact. The first Ming emperor was born into a poor family, and later became a monk. When he ascended the throne, he may have feared being deposed by someone of royal blood, or "real dragon." Therefore, he ordered bell towers built all over China to repress the "dragon spirits."

Forest of Steles

Xi'an

A STELE IS AN OBLONG SLAB of stone or terra-cotta, set upright, with inscriptions or relief carvings on its face. Such tablets are usually created to serve as monuments or commemorative stones, and have been found among the ancient ruins of Mesopotamian, Egyptian, Greek, and Mayan civilizations, as well as very prominently throughout China. The oldest, largest, and most famous collection of steles in China is known as the Forest of Steles, and is located at the foot of the south city wall of Xi'an, at the site of the old Shaanxi Provincial Museum.

The steles inscribed with the Confucian Classics were originally housed in the Imperial Academy in Chang'an (present-day Xi'an). In A.D. 904, the borders of Chang'an were redefined for military purposes, reduced in size. This left some important monuments outside the city's protection, so they were moved to the Wenxuan Temple. Then, in 1087, the Song Dynasty emperor Daozong had all the steles in the city moved to one place—the present site of the Forest of Steles—to shelter them from the weather. This site expanded through the Jin, Yuan, Ming, and Qing dynasties as additional steles were created, and in the early Qing Dynasty, the vast exhibit acquired the name Forest of Steles.

Today, the museum holds over two thousand steles, more than half of which can be viewed by the public. These are divided among seven exhibition halls, the most recent of which was established in 1982. The steles are of interest not only for their historical content, but also for the aesthetic appeal of the artwork and, especially, the calligraphy carved into them. There are five basic forms of calligraphic script—regular, cursive, running, seal, and clerical. The steles show that each of these forms has gained in simplicity and purity with the passage of time, outgrowing needless complexity.

The first exhibition hall contains the twelve Confucian Classics, which detail the philosophy of Confucius. These texts occupy 114 tablets—a massive undertaking ordered by Emperor Wenzong of the Tang Dynasty, to ensure that the texts would endure forever. The second hall features the famous Nestorian Stele, with its distinctive Christian cross on top. This tablet tells of the arrival of a Nestorian priest—representative of a Christian sect denounced as heretical by the Church—and the establishment of a chapel in 781. Other steles include the works of famous poets, a map of Chang'an during its golden period, and a collection of splendid line drawings.

For information about Hugh Lauter Levin Associates
publications, please refer to our web site, at:

http://www.HLLA.com